THINGS
WOMEN
DO TO
REALLY ANNOY
MEN

BY
TONI GOFFE

First published in Great Britain by
Pendulum Gallery Press
56 Ackender Road, Alton, Hants GU34 1JS

© TONI GOFFE 1995 1998

THINGS WOMEN DO TO
REALLY ANNOY MEN
ISBN 0-948912-32-4

PRINTED IN GREAT BRITAIN BY
UNWIN BROTHERS LTD, OLD WOKING, SURREY

HOW TO USE THIS BOOK

BUY IT , TAKE IT HOME AND
WHEN YOU'RE SITTING QUIETLY
WITH YOUR PARTNER, READ
IT TOGETHER AND DISCUSS IN
A FRIENDLY WAY WHICH OF
THESE ANNOYANCES APPLY TO
YOUR PARTNER AND WHAT ARE
THEY GOING TO DO ABOUT
THEM?
IF THIS APPEARS TO BE A LITTLE
ONE SIDED WHY DON'T YOU...
BUY BOTH BOOKS...
NOW YOU HAVE ONE EACH.
"THINGS MEN DO TO REALLY
ANNOY WOMEN" AND
"THINGS WOMEN DO TO
REALLY ANNOY MEN".

NOW YOU CAN DISCUSS WHAT
ANNOYS YOU BOTH ABOUT
EACH OTHER.
IT COULD BECOME AN
EXHILARATING EVENING
TO REMEMBER........

WOMEN INSIST YOU OPEN THE DOOR FOR THEM, THEN...

WOMEN NEVER BUY A ROUND...

WOMEN ALWAYS CHOOSE THE MOST EXPENSIVE
ITEM ON THE MENU...

THEY NEVER OFFER TO GO "DUTCH" WHEN THE BILL ARRIVES...

THEY SPEND HOURS AND HOURS IN THE
RESTAURANT TOILET...

IF A WOMEN INVITES YOU IN FOR A COFFEE,
IT'S ALWAYS WITH ALL HER FLAT MATES...

THEN...

THEY GET UPSET IF YOU SPEND ANY TIME IN THE PUB...

THEY ARE RELUCTANT TO ENTERTAIN YOUR FRIENDS
WHEN YOU GET HOME FROM THE PUB...

...THEN COMPLAIN WHEN YOU HAVEN'T WASHED UP...

THEY FILL YOU UP WITH FOOD THEN EXPECT YOU
TO HELP WASH UP...

THEY ALWAYS ASK YOU TO WASH UP WHEN YOU'RE MAKING SOME BIG ITEM FOR THE HOUSE...

ONCE COMFORTABLY SEATED ON THE COUCH, THEY EXPECT YOU TO JUMP UP AND HELP THEM AT A MOMENTS NOTICE...

WOMEN ALWAYS CHOOSE THE WRONG MOMENT
TO TALK TO YOU...

THEIR REQUESTS ARE UNREASONABLE...

...THEN THEY THREATEN TO LEAVE YOU...

WOMEN DON'T LIKE TO SEE YOU RELAXING...

THEY MAKE YOU DO SOMETHING YOU'RE NOT GOOD AT...
THEN MOCK YOU...

WOMEN WILL DO ANYTHING TO GET YOU TO GO SHOPPING...

...AND WHEN YOU DON'T...
THEY GO FOOD SHOPPING AND RETURN WITH FOUR DRESSES...

WOMEN LOVE SPENDING YOUR MONEY...

WOMEN ARE ILLOGICAL ABOUT MONEY...

WOMEN ALWAYS WANT TO STAY IN WHEN YOU WANT THEM TO GO OUT...

THEY ALWAYS CHANGE THEIR MINDS...

THEY DON'T UNDERSTAND WHY MEN PLAY GOLF...

WOMEN ALWAYS WANT TO WATCH THE WRONG FILMS ON TV...

WOMEN DON'T KNOW ABOUT CARS...

WOMEN THINK THEY CAN DRIVE BETTER THEN MEN...

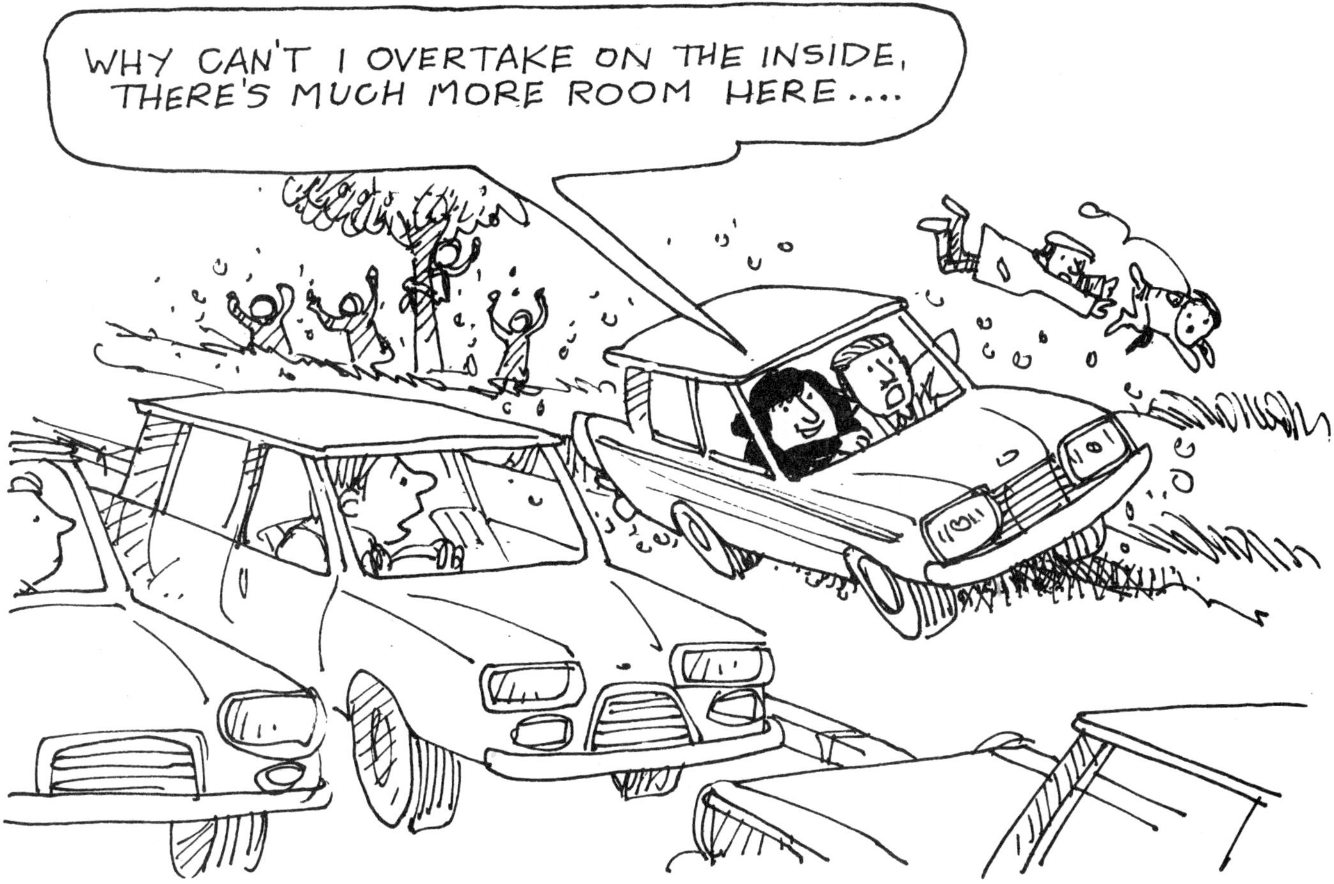
WHY CAN'T I OVERTAKE ON THE INSIDE,
THERE'S MUCH MORE ROOM HERE....

THEY NEVER TELL YOU WHEN THEY DAMAGE THE CAR...

CAR QUIZ: DOES YOUR FEMALE PARTNER DO
ANY OF THE FOLLOWING?

ALWAYS USE YOUR INTERIOR MIRROR TO PLUCK
HER EYEBROWS (WHILE YOU'RE DRIVING, OF COURSE)...

ALWAYS TELL YOU TO DRIVE "PROPERLY"...

TELLS YOU TO DRIVE MORE SMOOTHLY AS SHE PAINTS
HER FINGER NAILS...

DRIVES YOU MAD... AS SHE TRIES TO PARK BETWEEN
TWO CARS...

WHEN SHE'S DRIVING SWITCHES ON THE WINDSCREEN
WIPERS, WHEN SHE WANTS TO TURN RIGHT...

SHE CAN'T FIND THE CAR SHE LEFT IN THE CAR PARK...

MORE THINGS WOMEN DO IN CARS TO REALLY ANNOY YOU.

DOES YOUR PARTNER...

USE YOUR INTERIOR MIRROR TO PUT ON LIPSTICK...

TALK TO YOU WHEN YOUR TRYING TO CONCENTRATE...

IGNORE YOU WHEN YOUR TRYING TO TELL THEM
SOMETHING IMPORTANT...

INSIST ON PLAYING THEIR MUSIC ON YOUR
CASSETTE PLAYER...

AFTER SHOPPING, LEAVE IT IN THE CAR AND
EXPECTING YOU TO BRING IT IN THE HOUSE...

NEVER CLEAN THEIR MESS OUT OF YOUR CAR...

SAY "IT DOESN'T MATTER WHAT SORT OF CAR IT IS AS LONG
AS THE COLOUR MATCHES MY SHOES"...

WOMEN ARE ILLOGICAL...

WOMEN ARE DIFFICULT TO UNDERSTAND...

...THEY DO IT DELIBERATELY...

WOMEN ARE CONFUSING...

WOMEN WANT BABIES...

WOMEN ARE NEVER READY TO GO OUT...

WOMEN ONLY HAVE SEX WHEN THEY WANT TO...

WOMEN ARE PREDICTABLE.....

PENDULUM GALLERY PRESS

56 Ackender Road·Alton·Hants·GU34 1JS Fax & Telephone Alton (0420) 84483

DON'T FORGET TO ADD ON THE POSTAGE THANKS!

ORDER NOW!

PGP

SPORT			IBSN NO
JUDO FOR JUNIORS	....	£2.99	0.948912.01.4
JUDO GAMES	....	£2.99	0.948912.00.6

HUMOUR			
IS THERE SEX AFTER 40 FOR HER?	....	£2.99	0.948912.20.0
IS THERE SEX AFTER40 FOR HIM ?		£2.99	0.948912.19.0
ARE YOU FINISHED AT 50?	....	£2.99	0.948912.05.7
ARE YOU STILL FLIRTY AT 30?	....	£2.99	0.948912.06.5
THE VERY VERY SEXY ADULT DOT-TO -DOT BOOK		£2.99	0.948912.09.X
THE NEW SEX DIET	....	£2.99	0.948912.04.9
SEX AND YOUR STARS	....	£2.95	0.948912.08.1
HAPPY? BIRTHDAY	....	£2.99	0.948912.12.X
HAPPY? RETIREMENT	....	£2.99	0.948912.10.3
GET WELL SOON	....	£2.99	0.948912.15.4
FARTING!	....	£2.99	0.948912.17.0
GREENS ARE GOOD FOR YOU	....	£2.99	0.948912.13.8
CAN SEX IMPROVE YOUR GOLF?	....	£2.99	0.948912.18.9
IS THERE LIFE WITHOUT DOGS?	....	£2.99	0.948912.22.7
IS THERE LIFE WITHOUT CATS?	....	£3.90	0.948912.21.9
IS THERE LIFE AFTER 60?	....	£2.99	0.948912.24.3
IS THERE LIFE AFTER BABY?	....	£2.99	0.948912.23.5
IS THERE A LIFE LEFT FOR GRANDPARENTS?		£2.99	0.948912.25.1
WAS THERE LIFE BEFORE COMPUTERS?	....	£2.99	0.948912.26.X
WHY WHY D.I.Y.?	....	£2.99	0.948912.29.4
LIFE`S LESSONS FROM MY CAT	....	£2.50	0.948912.27.8
LIFE`S LESSONS FROM MY DOG	....	£2.50	0.948912.28.6
LOVE CATS	....	£2.50	0.948912.30.8
THINGS MEN DO TO REALLY ANNOY WOMEN		£2.99	0.948912.31.6
THINGS WOMEN DO TO REALLY ANNOY MEN		£2.99	0.948912.32.4

TO BUY THESE BOOKS YOU CAN EITHER ORDER FROM YOUR LOCAL BOOKSELLER OR
FROM US AT PENDULUM GALLERY PRESS·56 ACKENDER ROAD·ALTON·HANTS·GU341JS·
(PLEASE SEND £1 EXTRA TO COVER POSTAGE AND PACKAGING)